War 101

A behind-the-scenes look at war

by

Mike Bhangu

BBP

Library and Archives Canada Cataloguing in Publication

Bhangu, Mike Singh, author
    War 101 : a behind-the-scenes look at war / Mike Bhangu.

Includes bibliographical references and index.
Issued in print and electronic formats.
ISBN 978-1-988735-02-3 (softcover).--ISBN 978-0-9940799-6-1 (ebook)

    1. War. I. Title.

U21.2.B42 2017   **355.02**   **C2017-901992-9**
                                                        C2017-901993-7

Illustrator: Mike Bhangu
Published by BB Productions
British Columbia, Canada
thinkingmanmike@gmail.com

Table of Contents

Introduction

Sometimes, the causes of war are not what they're presented as. Sometimes, the narrative is like a sugar candy with a sour filled center. Sometimes, the people are misled to support war and soldier.

This manuscript briefly examines the beast that is war. In specific, the techniques able to persuade a person to support the evil, the distortions that motivate people to soldier, false flag operations, and the misrepresentation of right and wrong so to bring about war.

CHAPTER 1
ENGINEERED TO WAR

Why doesn't the word "war" trigger the mind to conjure ugly thoughts and images? Can it be that bloodshed is at the root of Western culture and government—seeded by Romulus and Remus and harvested by the British colonialists? Is this why the word "war" carries with it connotations of honour, virtue, and courage?

The word "war" is associated with ideas of honour, virtue, and courage. The word "war" can be associated with opposite notions, such as "murder" and "the devil", and to images akin to those shown by Spielberg in his movie, *Saving Private Ryan.* A different perception can be propagated. An accurate depiction can be given. But if this were done, the war-makers might not benefit.

War Propaganda

Fathomed by generations of political spin and deliberate deception, when the war-makers desire war, they tamper with the ideas of good and evil.

Warring-voters and narrow-minded soldiers, the two ingredients required to bake the contemporary war cake, but in the hearts of most women and men, bloodshed and murder have no place of rest. So, if the objective is to convince good people to support an evil such as war, the people must understand war as a requirement to safeguard against a greater darkness. Furthermore, the hostilities must be associated with a person's sense of right and to a higher purpose.

To accomplish this end, during times of war and the period leading up to war, ideas of good and evil, or right and wrong, are dictated to a nation's people. In the dictation, the opponent is typically depicted as evil personified (the other), and they as those draped in righteousness and good.

It's a common rendition. So common in fact that it's difficult to blame those who support war. They were trained to hum the tune by which they march.

The people of Nazi Germany were subject to information designed to accomplish the above. The Nazi Germans were indoctrinated to think they stood under the banner of righteous. In their minds, they were heroes.

The people of the Catholic Church were also subject to trickery. Of this, the Crusades are excellent examples. The different Popes of the day, and those in positions of power, during the Crusades, regularly misled their flock. The Catholics were taught that those who war against the Muslims and the Jews will gain entrance into heaven or their sins will be forgiven.

The Romans are another notable example. Almost every people they attacked were considered "evil barbarians".

The Americans too have utilized the language of deception. For example, during the Vietnam War, the Vietnamese were described as the unjust people. They were depicted as "the other" so to morally and intellectually justify invasion and murder to the American voter and soldier. And during the Cold War, the American people were indoctrinated to fear the U.S.S.R. They were taught that the Soviets did nothing but plot, day and night, to attack them. The people behind the Iron Curtain were depicted as strictly evil-doers.

Moscow sounded a very similar alarm. The only significant difference, the Americans were branded as the villains and those without a moral compass.

I guess this is the norm during times of war. Words are used as weapons. I guess it's easier to hurt another when the mind has condemned the other as morally and intellectually inhuman.

The practice of manipulating the ideas of right and wrong (good and evil) isn't a phenomenon of the contemporary world or something that Nazi Germany, the Vatican, Rome, America, or Russia invented. Rulers have manoeuvred the ideas of good and evil since the beginning of written history.

History has evolved to give the respect deserved by a saint to a sinner, to glorify dark behaviour such as murder, and to persuade people to internalize violence and realize that type of darkness. According to Grace M. Jantzen, in her book, *Foundations of Violence: Death and Displacement of Beauty* (2004), elements of culture and history are designed to persuade the common person to occasionally justify hurting another.

To this extent, popular culture daily communicates violent information. Television, film, video games, and music are plagued by violent behaviour and covered by a violent ethos. Even cartoons are subject to the backwardness. Perhaps, the war-makers understand the nature of the human. The earlier one is indoctrinated, the easier it is to convince him or her when the time is right for war.

For as long as written history can remember, the war-makers have influenced the masses to war. In the process, the ideas of right and wrong, or good and evil, are sometimes manoeuvred to convince good people to murder. Keep this in mind when the contemporary war-makers such as the Chicken-Hawks and the radical religious leaders attempt to sell their position. Keep this in mind when listening, reading, or watching.

The good in a person will not allow an individual to fire ammo at another human. But the good in a person can be buried underneath falsehood and rhetoric.

Deprivation

Deprivation serves a purpose and it benefits any nation-state that sanctions war. You see, a deprived person is more likely to soldier.

Poor people are easier to manipulate, and to satisfy their hunger pains, deprived people are more likely to compromise the integrity of the soul and to soldier. Without poor people, armies do not rise and fall.

Poverty has other benefits and poor people are more likely to break the law. This happening allows the ruling class an excuse to employ a police force, and since the rulers write the laws, in effect, the ruling class control those who police. The primary purpose of a policing agency is to maintain the status quo and to keep the rulers at the top of the power structure.

Policing agencies were not created to protect the people but to maintain law and order—laws created by and for the rulers. To justify the use of a police force, a certain level of wickedness must be evident amid the general public. And not surprisingly, after a careful historical analysis, when the ruling class turn against the people, they use a nation's police force like a "Don" who employs thugs and gangsters. Under that pretext, when the general public organize to improve their collective lot, the policing agencies are dispatched to break their movement.

Minions a police force can be and study Hitler's Germany if you don't believe, or travel to an underdeveloped country and see. In the less-developed nations, like weeds police corruption is.

Now, don't get me wrong. Those dispatched to attack a socially conscious movement are not bad people. In such a situation, by way of misinformation, they're typically taught that the movement is the evil and they the good.

This all said, in the Western World, police officers more so elevate the level of safety within communities than hinder social progress. I respect the work they do. Especially in the country I was born to, Canada. The growth of stable communities is dependent on them. Without police officers, there will be anarchy.

Poverty is required to persuade an individual to act as he or she normally wouldn't. However, deprivation alone isn't enough and the mind must be caged as the body is. The potential soldier must be desensitized to the suffering of other people, and the potential soldier must be indoctrinated and moulded into a predatory animal. Fortunately, the collective intelligence and the popular culture harbour a violent ethos and they successfully prepare a person to soldier.

Typically, when a war breaks loose, a small group of people want more than their share to eat and more beneath their feet.

Occupation of the Mind

If popular media hasn't accidentally revealed it yet, I'd like to share a little secret. Information can be structured to deceive the reader, viewer, or listener.

The deceptive techniques are many and what I repeatedly see while reading or watching are the employment of soft words, simple sentences, and well-spoken people to create an accepting and convincing picture. In the process, sometimes, the true root of a problem is left unsaid. For example, many people in the developed world understand the disposition of the Third World as self-inflicted. However, the current conditions of the Third World are a direct result of the colonial era and the type of economy this era forcefully instituted. It was a system that exploited a nation's labour, funnelled wealth to the top without distributing fairly, extracted a nation's resources without giving back the equivalent, and created the cash crop economy. The Third World is what it is because of the colonial age, but instead of seeing colonialism for what it was, most like to romanticize the notions of exploitation, murder, and looting.

In a sense, the Western World still oppresses less-developed nations. The West hinders their development by reducing their purchasing power and by offering economic options that don't benefit the underdeveloped.

Firstly, the international financial community devalues the currencies of the less-developed countries. This is done to diminish their purchasing power. A weak currency stifles the ability to purchase knowledge and technology from the developed world. Secondly, they force the underdeveloped to govern according to neo-liberal thought. That is, if the less-developed wish to access a highly valued international currency so to purchase knowledge and technology from the West. However, neo-liberalism doesn't help improve the living standard of a nation's people, and no Western nation advanced under the cloud of neo-liberal thought. Every single Western nation developed because of a strong and central government, and relative freedom from foreign interests.

Neo-liberal thought dictates that a strong and central government be weakened, barriers to international trade and capital—such as tariffs—be reduced or eliminated, and the private sector head a nation's development. In essence, neo-liberal thought strips a nation of her sovereignty and allows capital to influence the advancement of a country, and in most cases, it allows the developed world to exploit the people and the resources of the underdeveloped.

The Third World is coerced into accepting neo-liberalism through international organizations like the World Bank and the International Monetary Fund. They only lend money to the nations willing to surrender their sovereignty and their right to self-determination.

The countries that did institute neo-liberalism eventually reduced the amount of money spent on health, education, and clean water. Simultaneously, the cost of food and fuel irrationally increased.

Speaking of development, the progression of Israel is a notable example. Neither this nation nor any of her major infrastructures existed prior to World War II. But somehow, within 50 years, Israel has risen as an international powerhouse.

Israel is an international player, and after critically examining her establishment, it's clear that Israel didn't develop as other less-developed nations are forced to. Israel is a developed country because of American and British assistance, and more importantly, the autonomy and the sovereignty the international community permitted Israel to exercise.

The development of Israel should be used as an example and the methods obviously worked. Why aren't they utilized to help the less-developed progress?

The language of deliberate deception and political spin are a common occurrence. The conflict within the nation of Ireland, between the Catholics and the Protestants, is another example of circumstances propagated and perceived as self-inflicted. In actuality, it's more a conflict between the Scottish and the Irish than between religions. Sometime during the 16th century, in an attempt to create conflict amid the Irish and subdue their struggle for independence, the British Crown relocated a large number of Scots to Ireland. In view of the fact that the two held a conflictual history, naturally, the two started battling. The British colonialists were infamous for creating conflict. They behaved as if the world was their playground, and most of the places the British were colonizers in, were left in a state of disarray by the Red Coats.

Centuries have passed since the British first instigated the conflict, and the stories of hate received by each have accumulated and embedded themselves into each collective intelligence. Each psyche perceives the other as the evil, and tragically, most people do not know how to calculate the lowest common denominator to the problem.

The language of deliberate deception isn't a thing that died with colonialism. Even today, information is misrepresented so to disguise the true root of a problem. The invasion of Iraq is a prime example. There were no weapons of mass destruction in Iraq but the American people were told otherwise by the media. Under the impression that Saddam owned WMDs, the Americans invaded that country.

The reason for the invasion of Iraq is illegitimate but it was reported as legitimate. As such, the people were misled to support overseas bloodshed.

If popular media hasn't accidentally revealed it yet, I'd like to share a little secret. Information can be structured to deceive the reader, viewer, or listener, and a lie can be sold as a truth if presented and publicized as if it was.

Most of the information an individual absorbs comes from a few centralized sources, controlled by a handful of people. Unfortunately, for one reason or another, sometimes, the few masters of the media deliver information that's subjective, misleading, and irrelevant. If they don't want to be, the masters of the media don't have to be truthful, balanced, and objective. When they don't want to be, there is no manmade entity able to keep them in check.

The media industry doesn't exist to share information able to enhance the human experience. The media industry exists to make money. As such, the media communicates what the money dictates and they will never slap the hand that feeds.

False Flag Operations

Sometimes, those who control the means to fabricate an "artificial truth" do, and sometimes, violent measures are used to substantiate the "artificial truth".

During her days as an empire, the British Crown mastered the art. They readily lied, incited trouble, and manufactured events so to justify attacking another people.

The British Imperialists weren't the only who exercised this war strategy, and according to the book edited and published by Hephaestus Books, *Articles on False Flag Operations* (2011), it's an old tactic. On numerous occasions, by many different groups, fabrications were used as an excuse to war. The operational-term, False Flag, is commonly used to denote the stratagem. For example:

Mukden Incident (1937)
Japan fabricated the kidnapping of a Japanese soldier and blamed China. Japan used the incident to justify the invasion of that country.

Shelling Incident (1939)
The Russian army shelled a Russian village, which bordered Finland, and then blamed the attack on Finland. The incident was used by Russia to justify the 1939 Winter War.

Gleiwitz Incident (1939)

Germany manufactured evidence to persuade the German people to war against Poland. Germany even went to the extent of killing her own people and blaming the Polish for the murders.

The Lavon Affair Incident (1954)

So to convince the British to maintain a military presence in Egypt, Israel planned to create instability within that country by bombing British civilians and then accusing the Muslim Brotherhood for the attack. The operation was a complete failure. The Israeli Defense Minister, Pinhas Lavon, was forced to exit public office because of the botched operation.

Operation Northwoods Incident (1962)

The U.S. Department of Defence conceptualized the operation as a means to persuade the American voter to support a war with Cuba. The aim was to overthrow Fidel Castro. The plan focused toward attributing violent behaviour to Cuba and against America. Suggestions such as sinking a U.S. ship and blaming Cuba, harassing American aircraft with jets disguised as Cuban MiGs, and manufacturing attacks on U.S soil, by Cubans, were considered. The operation was inevitably rejected by President John F. Kennedy.

Sometimes, those who control the means to fabricate an "artificial truth" do. Within the context of this manuscript, it's typically done to depict another group as a threat and an evil. It's an old tactic. Create a conflict and offer the solution. We will never truly know when the idea was first practiced. Only one thing is certain. This sort of corrupt behaviour is a reality. As such, a person should not be afraid to reasonably and critically contemplate violent incidences that lead to war.

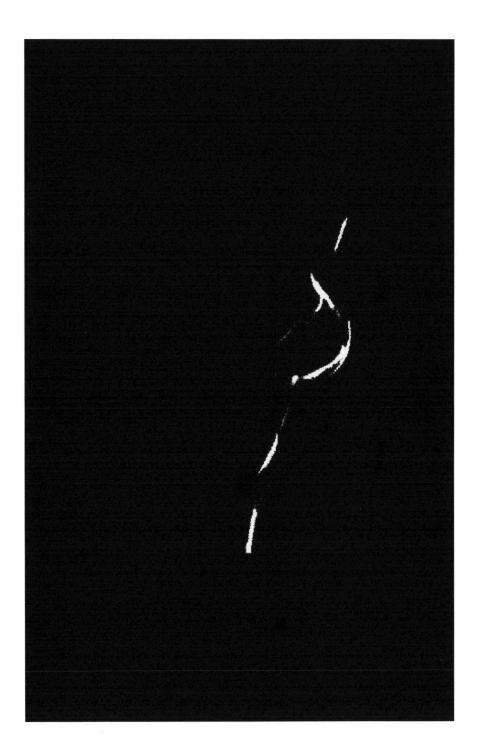

Assassin

As written in Marco Polo's journal, there once was a Persian cult leader named Hasan as-Sabah, and he was able to persuade a devote Muslim to commit murder.

Hasan was a very cunning man. To convince a person to assassinate another human, he utilized the afterlife. Hasan would drug a man unconscious and have him carried into an amazingly beautiful garden—a place designed to mimic the Islamic notion of Heaven. When the man would awake, typically, he would mistake the garden for Paradise. After giving him a few moments to absorb the experience, Hasan, disguised as some sort of angelic messenger, would appear to the man. At which time, Hasan would weave a web of lies and convince the man that the only means to stay in Heaven involved killing a particular someone.

The men recruited by Hasan were considered the most dangerous type of assassin. They didn't care if they died while fulfilling the duties of a murderer. In their minds, killing another came with a free pass into Heaven.

In the 1260s, Hulagu Khan, the grandson of Genghis, destroyed Hasan and his garden.

Although the garden is no more, there's still something the modern person can learn from the deception. Trust no one, despite the reward, if he or she tries to instigate murder.

Reason

Reasoning has done astronomical amounts of damage. It spilt blood in Jerusalem, it depicted the African-American as inferior, and it promoted the British Monarchs as more than mortal. Irrational thought still plagues us today. Equality is still a dream, the holy still stand on opposite ends, and the person is still repressed.

And how does reasoning damage? Well, the mind can think inconclusive thoughts are conclusive—it can trick itself. Even when thoughts conclude that flying buffalo live in Singapore or Saddam hid weapons of mass destruction in Iraq.

You see, the ability to reason is double-sided and very much neutral and subjective. Not only is reason an ability, reasoning (to make logical associations), reason is also a tool like an internet search engine. It searches through the information stored within the human condition, pulls information relevant to the problem at hand, and then communicates that information to the time and space of thought. Naturally, it can only gather information that's available, and only the information gathered by reason will be reasoned and used to influence the mapping of metaphysical and physical motions.

The point I'm trying to make is that information dictates the length of reason's chain. The more truthful information an individual contains, the less restrictive the chain becomes. The less restrictive the chain, the more conclusive become thoughts, and in turn, actions.

Known or not, the information a person absorbs naturally influences a person's thoughts and actions. So, it just might matter what the built world tells and shows. If the built world only tells and shows half the information, only half the information will be absorbed. The outcome will be a person who knows only half the alphabet and lives in the land of sentences, words, and letters.

Reason II

The murder of the Indigenous, the witch-trials of Salem, and the looting of Punjab by the British. An enemy a thought can be if a thought is unfinished.

It's like looking at the world wearing the wrong prescription glasses and not knowing it—the distorted view might seem accurate. Under such conditions, the information the mind works with is limited, and naturally, the conclusions the mind reaches will be inconclusive. However, the mind might not realize it and the conclusions might be understood as conclusive.

Conclusions represented as such are most dangerous. They can inspire the wicked within the person and they're able to justify letting the wicked within out. How else were the atrocities of the Inquisitions and the murder of the Indigenous reasoned? What else explains the idiots, the asses, and the immoral motions as those of the colonial era?

Even-handedly, the potential for reason to misdirect a person isn't limited to a certain demographic or nation. We're all subject to the human condition's weakness and it's impossible for any person to know everything. Nevertheless, it's still possible to do something about this unfortunate disposition.

Luckily, the design of the person comes with cognitive agents able to restrain reason. When reasoning, rely on empathy and compassion to judge conclusions. Even if thoughts are unfinished and the mind perceives otherwise, empathy and compassion will prevent a person from injuring another human. The mistakes that hurt another are the worst mistakes a person can make.

The murder of the Indigenous, the witch-trials of Salem, and the looting of Punjab by the British. An enemy a thought can be if a thought is unfinished.

Freedom-Fighter or Terrorist?

Sometimes, to the detriment of the righteous, the freedom-fighter is labelled a terrorist. I cannot be certain who is and who isn't, but I am sure of one occasion. In the 1980s and 1990s, the honourable Sikh nation was attacked by the Indian Government and then branded as terrorists.

In 1984, with the assistance of the British and the Russian Governments, on the anniversary of the Fifth Sikh Master's martyrdom, Guru Arjan,[1] the Indian army attacked the Golden Temple Complex, the holiest Sikh place of worship. They assaulted the complex under the guise of hunting "so-called" terrorists. In the process, they burned the Sikh Reference Library,[2] used artillery to blast holes through the Golden Temple, and murdered innocent women and children—who were in the complex to attend the anniversary of Guru Arjan's martyrdom.[3]

> *"A singer at the Golden Temple, Harcharan Singh Ragi, his wife and their young daughter came out of their quarters near the information office on June 6 afternoon. They witnessed the killings of hundreds of people, including women, and would themselves have been shot if a commander had not taken pity on their young daughter who fell at his feet begging him to spare her parents' lives."[4]*

"A woman school teacher, Ranbir Kaur, witnessed the shooting of another group of 150 persons whose hands had been tied behind their backs with their own turbans."[5]

"Children were lined up and shot in the Golden Temple by army officials."[6]

With the destruction of the Reference Library, lost were hundreds of paintings, tens-of-thousands of books, hundreds of relics, rare hukamnamas, over two thousand manuscripts of *Guru Granth Sahib Ji,* and newspapers stemming back to 1876.

The Indian Government's excuse for the attack entails neutralizing "so-called" terrorists hiding inside. However, other means were available instead of attacking the Golden Temple, the holiest place of the Sikhs, on a holy day. It's more likely they assaulted the Golden Temple not to neutralize terrorists but to strike fear into the minds of all Sikhs. They were attempting to send a message to the Sikh people, and if the Sikhs continued questioning government corruption, punishment will ensue. This would explain why the Indian Government executed innocent women and children. This would explain why they burned rare manuscripts. This would explain why they attacked the most sacred symbol of the Sikhs, on a sacred day.

The Indian Government aimed to intimidate the Sikhs because the Sikhs were questioning government corruption. The Sikhs were demanding better social, economic, religious, and political conditions within the land of a million martyrs, Punjab. Several of the demands are outlined in the *Anandpur Resolution of 1973*.

Now, even though the initiatives were smaller in scope, the attack on the Golden Temple Complex wasn't the first hostile act the Indian Government is guilty of. They initiated the campaign of intimidation several years prior.

Before the attack on the Golden Temple Complex, for several years, the Indian Government harassed, falsely imprisoned, tortured, and murdered dozens upon dozens of Sikhs. Individuals such as Amarjeet Singh Daheru, Baljeet Singh Sultanpur, Kashmir Singh Ladhwal, and Bhola Singh were all executed in fake police encounters. Punjab Police Officers were the principle goons who undertook the immoral campaign of intimidation. As reported by *"Night and Day News"*, 2013, Punjab Police Officer, Surjit Singh, confessed to unjustly killing over 83 Sikhs. He further implicates numerous other officers. Jaswant Singh Khalra, a Sikh activist, before his assassination by the Punjab Police, uncovered evidence linking police officers to tens-of-thousands of Sikh murders.

The attack toward the Sikh people stretched over many years until, eventually, the Indian Government declared a civil war. Interestingly, before the Indian Government unleashed hell in 1984, they planned for a civil war years prior, and they actually spent the time and the resources to build a life size replica of the Golden Temple Complex—in which the military rehearsed the attack. However, India sells a different story. They imply the assault wasn't much planned but more of a spontaneous act to capture terrorists. Unfortunately, by constructing a replica, and taking the time to work with foreign governments, the Indian Government demonstrated their premeditated intent.

The Sikhs eventually learnt of the planned attack, and through public speeches made by individuals such as Jarnail Singh, the Sikhs warned the Indian Government that if they attacked, the Sikh nation will defend itself. The "so-called" terrorists within the complex were there to defend the Golden Temple. A General in the Indian army defected, Shahbeg Singh, one of the greatest Indian military minds of the 20th century, and he was instrumental in defending Harmunder Sahib (the Golden Temple).

In retaliation for the honourless attack on the Golden Temple, the murder of the innocent, and the destruction of Sikh literature, two Sikhs murdered the Prime Minister of India, Indira Gandhi. After the murder of Indira, leading politicians from the Congress Party used the incident to further their agenda of terror and intimidation. They organized the 1984 anti-Sikh terror campaign,[7] and using voter lists, they systematically attacked Sikh households and businesses.[8] It's estimated that 10 000 Sikhs were massacred during the campaign.[9]

"For three days, gangs of arsonists and killers, in criminal collusion with the police and Congress politicians, who pointed out the houses of Sikhs, were allowed to rampage freely...No one was ever brought to trial."[10]

"By all responsible accounts the government calmly stood by even when several of its functionaries led the killing mobs on the streets."[11]

"The government controlled television Doordarshan, and the All India Radio began broadcasting provocative slogans seeking bloody vengeance, 'khoon ka badla khoon se lenge (Blood for blood!)'. Murderous gangs of 200 or 300 people led by the leaders, with policemen looking on, began to swarm into Sikh houses, hacking the occupants to pieces, chopping off the heads of children, raping women, tying Sikh men to tires set aflame with kerosene, burning down the houses and shops after ransacking them. Mobs stopped buses and trains, in and out of Delhi, pulling out Sikh passengers to be lynched to death or doused with kerosene and burnt alive."[12]

During the riots, to encourage the public, the government even went to the extent of exploiting the power of Bollywood. According to a witness, Jagdish Kaur, allegedly, Amitabh Bachchan, through a televised message, provoked the public to riot and attack the Sikhs. Supposedly, he perpetuated the slogan, *"khun ka badla khun sae laengae" (Blood for blood).*[13]

Although the anti-Sikh campaign ended within a few days, state-sponsored terrorism didn't. The campaign of terror and intimidation continued.   Firstly, the Indian Government persisted to label baptized Sikhs as terrorists, even though they were the group repeatedly attacked. They then used those sorts of operational-terms to violently occupy Punjab with 500 000 Indian troops.[14]   The occupation led to the deaths of 250 000 Sikhs.[15] From the year 1984 to approximately 1992, the Indian military targeted and killed anyone they wished, including innocent women and children.[16]

To this effect, special police units were established to terrorize civilians.[17] Abduction squads were created to target baptized Sikh men.[18] The Punjab Police illegally held, tortured, and/or murdered[19] any Sikh who might forward the idea of Sikh autonomy to cure the poor conditions of Punjab. Thousands upon thousands were secretly executed and cremated by the Punjab Police.[20] And military and police units regularly burglarized Sikh households.   They would accuse a Sikh family of harbouring a terrorist, and under this pretext, they would force the family from their home and then rob the family of their valuables.

So to depict the Sikhs as aggressors and not the victims, the Indian Government also committed acts of terror, through their agents, and then attributed those acts to the Sikhs. It's an old trick used by many past and present governments, and the Indian Government is well known for her honourless tactics. The Indians readily *"destabilize minority populations, provoke them into violence and then crack down on them."[21]*

But even more detrimental to the Sikh nation than the murder of the masses, during the violent occupation of Punjab, the Indian Government, through the media, lied to the Indian people and the international community. Domestically and on the world scene, the Sikhs were falsely depicted as the troublemakers and the Indian Government showcased herself as the victim of senseless Sikh violence. Before, during, and after the violent occupation of Punjab by the Indian Government, the Indian Government engaged in a disinformation campaign that falsely characterized the Sikhs as terrorists. Sadly, the consequences of their disinformation are yet to wash away.

In places the Sikhs immigrated to, such as Canada, they tried to organize and publicize the plight of the Sikh people living in Punjab. Unfortunately, the Indian Government was much more cunning than the Sikhs and the Indian Government readily planted pretenders amid them. These pretenders would disrupt the work. The Indians also bribed the Sikh leadership, those they could, to mislead and corrupt their people. Canadian law enforcement officers and agencies discovered that several Sikhs were paid by the Indian Government to monitor other Sikhs, and certain Punjabi newspapers in Canada were bought-off by the Indian Government. They were purposely publishing disinformation and depicting the Sikhs as hooligans. Concurrently, they were not reporting or spinning the atrocities committed by the Indian Government.[22]

When the Sikhs, in places such as Canada, did manage to publicly protest against the Indian Government's inhuman behaviour, the Indians would again outwit the Sikhs. They would sponsor counter-demonstrations designed to instigate violence and muddy the message the demonstrators were attempting to communicate.[23]

There is no question, on multiple fronts, the Indian Government attacked the Sikh nation. There is no question, without remorse, the Indian Government murdered innocent men, women, and children. Moreover, it's clear they endeavoured to neutralize a potential Sikh revolution, and it's clear they spread disinformation and depicted the victims as the villains. Unless of course, the quarter-million people they murdered were all terrorists.

However, if there were 250 000 people, or even half this number, willing to rebel against the state, obviously, the mechanisms designed to address the concerns of the people failed. Obviously, if a large number of people are willing to oppose the state, something isn't right with the conditions the people exist in. In most cases, if the conditions allow people to acquire the basics free of unreasonable restraints, and if the people's social and safety needs are met, the masses do not rebel.

We must understand that people are hesitant to rebel, especially when the opponent is significantly more powerful as the Indian Government was and is. In circumstances when the opponent is so powerful, confrontation isn't typically the first option.

After the independence of India, the Indian Government attacked the Sikh nation so to reduce their collective power. Today, Punjab is in shambles. The cost of hardship and a government turned on her people have taken a toll. Poverty, depression, liquor, drugs, corruption, and illiteracy are some of the ills that plague and the Sikh nation slowly falls.

Maybe, if the Indian Government didn't misuse and abuse the word "terrorist", the world might see the beauty in a rebuilt Sikh nation. Perhaps, if the world knew the truth, they might assist. Maybe, if the truth was popular, for their domestic acts of terror, the international community might hold the Indian Government accountable.

....

It becomes more than evident, after reviewing the print news from the 80s and 90s, reporters from the West were tricked by the Indian Government. They were conned to publicize misinformation and wrongly label the fighter of freedom a terrorist. And let's not forget that the British Government also participated in the honourless attack. I'm sure they too played a role in the international disinformation campaign.

The consequences of this campaign still haunt the Sikh people. Even still, the Western media occasionally associates the word "terrorist" with those who fought to defend the Sikh people. And the genocide-deniers in India still label. Anyone who writes or speaks about the 250 000 people who no longer live is labelled a Sikh separatist, a violent revolutionist, or a civil disturbance.

Freedom-Fighter or Terrorist?: Endnotes

1. Harnik Deol, <u>Religion and Nationalism in India: the case of the Punjab</u> (Routledge: London, 2000), p. 107.

2. Ibid., p. 108.

3. Martha Crenshaw, <u>Terrorism in Context</u> (Penn State Press: Pennsylvania, 1995), p. 385.

4. Amrik Singh and Ram Narayan Kumar, <u>Reduced to Ashes: The Insurgency and Human Rights in Punjab</u> (South Asia Forum for Human Rights: Nepal, 2003), p. 38.

5. Ibid.

6. Veena Das, <u>Life and Words: violence and the descent into the ordinary</u> (University of California Press: California, 2007), p. 130.

7. Harnik Deol, <u>Religion and Nationalism in India: the case of the Punjab</u> (Routledge: London, 2000), p. 109.

8. Om Gupta, <u>Encyclopedia of India, Pakistan and Bangladesh</u> (Isha Books: India, 2006), p. 131.

9. Harnik Deol, <u>Religion and Nationalism in India: the case of the Punjab</u> (Routledge: London, 2000), p. 109.

10. Thomas R. Metcalf, <u>A Concise History of Modern India</u> (Cambridge University Press: United States, 2006), p. 259.

11. P Lalan Tiwari, <u>Issues in Indian Politics</u> (Mittal Publications: New Delhi, India, 1995), p. 276.

12. Amrik Singh and Ram Narayan Kumar, <u>Reduced to Ashes: The Insurgency and Human Rights in Punjab</u> (South Asia Forum for Human Rights: Nepal, 2003), p. 42-43.

13. The Times of India. [https://timesofindia.indiatimes.com/india/1984-riots-Why-nobody-noticed-Amitabh-Bachchan-spewing-venom-in-India/articleshow/10429011.cms], May 2018.

14. Gerald James Jarson, <u>India's Agony over Religion</u> (SUNY Press: United States, 1995), p. 240.

15. Gus Martin, <u>Understanding Terrorism: Challenges, Perspectives, and Issues</u> (Sage Publications: United States, 2009), p. 190.

16. Martha Crenshaw, <u>Terrorism in Context</u> (Penn State Press: Pennsylvania, 1995), p. 396.

17. Jeffrey A. Sluka, <u>Death Squad: the anthropology of state terror</u> (University of Pennsylvania Press: Philadelphia, Pennsylvania, 2000), p. 209-210.

18. Ibid., p. 212-214.

19. Ibid., p. 220 - 222.

20. Amrik Singh and Ram Narayan Kumar, <u>Reduced to Ashes: The Insurgency and Human Rights in Punjab</u> (South Asia Forum for Human Rights: Nepal, 2003), p. 28-29.

21. Brian McAndrew and Zuhair Kasmeri, <u>Soft Target: the real story behind the Air India disaster</u> (James Lorimer &Company Ltd, Toronto, 2005), p. 35.

22. Ibid., p. 31.

23. Ibid.

The Saint-Soldier

Sometimes, a noble army rises. Sometimes, the righteous ones come together and battle the wicked. Among the Sikh people can be found such an organization, and amid them is the greatest covenant of the past 1000 years, the Khalsa. Established in 1699 by the Great Gobind Singh, the Khalsa is an armed union that exists for the purpose of defending against all tyrannical powers, protecting dharma, and protecting the holy of all religions—without taking anything in return. To this effect, death is a companion of the Singh (a member of the Khalsa). There is no compromising. Puran Singh, a renowned Sikh academic writes in his book, *Spirit of the Sikh*:

> *"Death, apparent death, is embraced by The Khalsa as no lover ever embraced his sweetheart. The Khalsa dies like the dashing waves of the sea, creating in the wake of its death millions more like itself. The life-breath of The Khalsa thus is losing its apparent life to gain its life everlasting."*

> *"In the ideal of The Khalsa, one can see the Ideal spirit of the passionate love of death for the sale of life as is seen in the Bushido of the Samurai of Old Japan. In that fervour of Yamoto, the physical life turns all into a little moth flickering its wings in infinite impatience to die. Death is the bride of the brave."*

Max Arthur McAuliffe, in his book, *The Sikh Religion: Volume 1*, writes, "*...no superiority of the enemies in number, no shot, no shell, can make his heart quail, since his Amrit (baptism) binds him to fight single-handed against millions.*" Rightfully so, the tyrants of the world are as strong as a million giants, and those brave enough to stand against them like the Biblical "David". Only without fear, and a will to sacrifice everything worldly, can the giants be defeated.

Not only is the Khalsa a community of warriors, the Khalsa is also a community of saints. Each member is humble, kind, gentle, loving, peaceful, fearless, forgiving, God-oriented, communally aware, soft-spoken, rational, truthful, mentally disciplined, knowledgeable, poetic, worldly, and detached from the self and Maya. The Khalsa only unsheathes the sword as a shield and not for secular gain. Puran Singh once wrote:

> *"Once it is said The Khalsa occupied the throne of Delhi when the Mughal Emperor submitted and acknowledged the power of The Khalsa, the leader Jassa Singh said— 'Ah! The Khalsa is atit (untouched by Maya). What has it to do with thrones'—and gave the throne back to the Mughals."*

> *"No one need be afraid of The Khalsa of Guru Gobind Singh, that it would ever think of seeking the bones of material objects. The eyes of The Khalsa are fixed heavenward."*

As dictated by Guru Gobind Singh to the great Sikh scholar, Bhai Nand Lal Goya, Goya writes in his book, *Tankhahnama*:

> *"The Khalsa is he who protects the poor, who destroys the wicked, who recites the Name, who fights the enemy, who concentrates his mind on the Name, who is detached from all other ties, who rides the horse, who fights every day, who bears arms, who promotes dharam, and who dies for his faith."*

The famous Sikh historian, Rattan Singh Bhangu, writes in his book, *Pracheen Panth Prakash*, the following on the Khalsa's creation.

> *"The perfect Guru, the Tenth, created the Khalsa Panth in this manner, so that they must wage a war against oppression."*

Guru Gobind Ji further describes the Khalsa as *"he is whose heart burns unflickering the Lamp of Naam, day and night, know him the Khalsa, the pure!"* As recorded by Puran Singh.

This connection to the essence of God is the reason the Khalsa's history is full of Singhs able to overcome incredible odds and achieve superhuman deeds, akin to those performed by Banda Singh, Deep Singh, Hari Singh, and Jassa Singh. As the Jedi draws power from the Force, the Singh draws power from the Lamp of Naam (the Primal Energy that pervades within all known and unknown).

An 18th century Muslim historian, and an enemy of the Sikhs, Qazi Nur Mohammad, once wrote of the Khalsa and the Khalsa's spirit:

"Do not call the Sikhs dogs, because they are lions and are courageous like lions in the battlefield. How can a hero, who roars like a lion be called a dog? Like lions they spread terror in the field of battle. If you wish to learn the art of war, come face to face with them in the battlefield. They will demonstrate it to you in such a way that one and all will shower praise on them. If you wish to learn the science of war, O swordsman, learn from them. They advance at the enemy boldly and come back safely after action. Understand; Singh is their title, a form of address for them. It is not justice to call them dogs; if you do not know Hindustani language, then understand that the word 'Singh' means a lion.

Truly, they are lion in battle, and at times of peace, they surpass in generosity. When they take the Indian sword in their hands they traverse the country from Hind to Sind. None can stand against them in battle, howsoever strong he may be. When they handle the spear, they shatter the ranks of the enemy. When they raise the heads of their spears towards the sky, they would pierce even through the Caucasus. When they adjust the strings of the bows, place in them the enemy killing arrows and pull the strings to their ears, the body of the enemy begins to shiver with fear. When their battle axes fall upon the armour of their opponents, their armour becomes their coffin.

The body of every one of them is like a piece of rock and in physical grandeur every one of them is more than fifty men. It is said that Behram Gore killed wild asses and lions. But if he were to come face to face with them even he would bow before them. Besides usual arms, they take their guns in hand and come into the field of action jumping and roaring like lions and raise slogans. They tear asunder the chests of many and shed blood of several in the dust. You say that musket is a weapon of ancient times, it appears to be a creation of these dogs rather than Socrates. Who else than these dogs can be adept in the use of muskets. They do not bother even if there are innumerable muskets. To the right and the left, in front and towards the back, they go on operating hundreds of muskets angrily and regularly.

...Besides their fighting, listen to one more thing in which they excel all other warriors. They never kill a coward who is running away from the battlefield. They do not rob a woman of her wealth or ornaments whether she is rich or a servant. There is no adultery among

these dogs, nor are they mischievous people... There is no thief amongst these dogs, nor is there amongst them any mean people. They do not keep company with adulaters'... Now that you have familiarised yourself with the behaviour of the Sikhs, you may also know something about their country. They have divided Punjab amongst themselves and have bestowed it upon every young and old." — Jang Namah (1765)

Jang Namah is an eye-witness account of Ahmed Shah Durrani's invasion of Punjab, in the year 1764. Commissioned by Ahmed Shah, the author naturally compromises objectivity when describing events and the people the Afghans invaded. When reading his work, it's clear Nur Mohammed held a strong prejudice toward the Sikhs. He refers to them as dogs, dirty idolaters, fire worshippers, etc. Nevertheless, even with his biases, he was unable to prevent his pen from glorifying the Khalsa and the Khalsa's members.

Jang Namah also shares the story of Baba Gurbakhsh Singh Shaheed and the 30 Singhs who battled 30 000 Afghanies. The 31 fought to prevent the desecration of the Golden Temple.

The true Singh, a replica of Gobind, is able to harness Naam because those who serve the Khalsa serve God. The Khalsa is a union of the Pure (the spiritually liberated), and sanctioned by The Lord for the purpose of ushering in the "Kingdom of God". An era on earth the Singhs call the "Khalsa Raj", in which God, truth, equality, justice, freedom, and righteousness prevail. It's said that so long as the Singh is true to the principles of the Khalsa, God will protect the Singh. However, The Great Architect is quick to abandon those who forget.

According to author, Narain Singh, in his book, *Guru Gobind Singh Re-told*, a year prior to the creation of the Khalsa, Guru Gobind withdrew into the Naina Devi Hills to meditate. He sought to connect with God and request The Eternal's guidance. He was troubled by the fact that he was forced to resort to violence to combat violence. He was aware that aggression is an evil which destroys human values and an idea that contradicts the core teachings of Sikhie—love and non-violence. However, the Mughal Administration, in their quest to convert all of India to Islam, unleashed hell on the people of Hindustan. Only those who unsheathed the sword were able to retain their non-Islamic identity. Guru Gobind unsheathed out of necessity, and even though each battle resulted in his victory, he fully recognized that violence is unbecoming.

Gobind eventually united with The Formless One, and after his union, Gobind proclaimed, as written in his book, *Bachittar Natak*:

> *"The Lord has sent me into the world for the purpose of spreading Dharma. He said to me, 'Go and spread Dharma (righteousness) everywhere, seize and smash the evil doers.' Know ye holy men, I have come solely*

for the purpose of bringing about Dharma, saving holy
men and completely uprooting wicked men. "

After his union, Guru Gobind established the Khalsa and initiated the quest to restore the conditions of an honourable existence. Conceived as a champion of dharma, the Khalsa is sanctioned by The Eternal to unsheathe but only in the face of extreme evil, and when peace is useless.

Sometimes, a noble army rises. Sometimes, the righteous ones come together and battle the wicked. Among the Sikh people can be found such an organization, and amid them is the greatest covenant of the past 1000 years, the Khalsa. Established in 1699 by the Great Gobind Singh, the Khalsa is an armed union that exists for the purpose of defending against all tyrannical powers, protecting dharma, and protecting the holy of all religions—without taking anything in return. To this effect, death is a companion of the Singh. There is no compromising.

....

"Says Kabeer, those humble people become pure - they become
Khalsa - who know the Lord's loving devotional worship.||4||3||" —
Ang 655 of 1430, Sri Guru Granth Sahib Ji

The Immaculate Junzi: Gobind

The ideal Philosopher-King.

The perfect Holy-Trooper.

The uncorrupted Warrior-Poet.

The alpha Saint-Soldier.

....

The day Gobind Singh was born, the holyman, Sayid Bhikhan Shah, proclaimed to his disciples, *"This day, a spiritual sovereign of immense magnificence has been born to illuminate the world..."*

Warrior-Poet

The one with a humorous and sweet tongue, a lion's heart, a worldly outlook, and a link to God.

The one with a philosopher king's mentality, a saint's humility, the compassion and honour of Saladin, and who serves humanity like Jassa Singh.

The one who lives to die for the greater good, journeys within the material world but is detached from, exists in the absolute realm, and cherishes truth, knowledge, virtue, and freedom.

The one whose strength is gained from Naam, whose mind's eye is with God, whose spirit is ironclad, and whose essence is the weak person's to command.

The one mesomorphic as the male offspring of Cronus—the Titan, quick as those who sprint the 100 meter in under 10 seconds, enduring as a marathon champion, and athletic as a multi-event gold medal Olympian.

This is a Warrior-Poet. This is a Singh.

....

"The Khalsa has no selfish ends for the aggrandisement of his small self in this warfare of life, because his 'I' has already grown by the Grace of the Guru to be the large 'I' of Humanity itself..." — Puran Singh

When to Unsheathe

Sin is silence when virtue is under bombardment and none show defiance. The art of violence is sanctioned but only if guided by the undying star of righteousness.

....

Regardless if death is a possibility, Guru Gobind's Khalsa is unflinching. Can you imagine the Master of War, in his grave, rolling? Sun only warred if he was assured victory. He never tasted the unseen reality—the precepts that govern the all encompassing. Hence, the greatest death is that of a shaheedi—the brave souls who perish battling tyranny.

Violence

The Khalsa's philosophy is centered on the idea of non-violence and love, but the Khalsa's philosophy also addresses violence.

The use of violence was introduced under extreme evil conditions and out of necessity—the sword was unsheathed to defend against Mughal extremism and irrationality. Mughal extremists viewed all non-Muslims as infidels and not worthy of life. Only those who converted to Islam, paid a tax, or were able to defend him or herself by way of violent means survived. This said, the introduction of violence came with guidelines.

Under the star of righteousness, violence can be employed but only if non-violence is ineffective, and if facing the likes of the Minotaur—a savage beast who senselessly ripped apart and devoured any human life he encountered. Outside this arena, peace and love are the swords used to combat and live. This is the way of the Singh.

The Brutish British

Most people in the developed world romanticize colonial intentions. This is so because the history books are too often silent.

The colonial era was an age of evil and there are many instances of the darkness. The colonialists, such as the French and the British, destroyed advanced people and places. The foremost example is the destruction of the Sikh Empire by the British.

> A Swiss officer and employee of the East India Company, Colonel A.L.H Polier, once wrote of the Sikh Empire: *"few countries can vie with theirs..."*

After much hardship and countless battles, the Sikh people of India defeated the Mughal Empire and then the Afghan invaders. By the early 1700s, the Khalsa, led by Banda Singh, built the foundation of the Sikh Empire and introduced such things as land reform and the first Sikh currency—primarily in Punjab, India. At this time, the Sikhs were divided into 12 or 13 Sikh unions. By the year 1799, under the guidance of Maharaja Ranjit Singh (the Lion of Punjab), the Sikh unions were consolidated and the Sikh Empire officially arose. It was an empire recognized by the British[1] and the Chinese. The Khalsa and the office of the Chinese Emperor signed a peace-treaty in the year 1842, September.

Unfortunately, even though the British recognized the Sikh Empire, the British imperial agenda could not permit a noble and advanced nation to exist, the British could not help but eye the Sikh Empire's resources, and the British agenda beckoned for control over as much of the earth as possible—regardless of who stood in the way. In the year 1849, the second major attempt by the British to defeat the Sikh army, the Khalsa, so to control the Sikh Empire, was a narrow success.

Although the British were victorious, they knew the Sikhs would not accept foreign rule. It was only a matter of time before the Khalsa reorganized and retook their homeland. So, the British agreed to hold the Sikh Empire in trust, until Ranjit Singh's only remaining son came of age to mediate the affairs of the Sikh Empire.

The Sikh nation-state was the last to fall to British imperialism in India, and only after the death of Maharaja Ranjit Singh. After which, poor leadership, internal conflict, and treason eventually gave rise to the conditions necessary for the British to defeat the Khalsa. I can't stress enough, if not for the traitors (Sikh pretenders), the Khalsa would not have fallen.

Not surprisingly, the traitors were from the elite class—the rich Sikhistanis. They desired the defeat of the empire, which was dominated by the Khalsa,[2] because it restricted them from increasing their personal wealth and status. They thought that if the Khalsa, and by extension, the virtues of the Khalsa were no more, they might freely fatten their profiles. For example, Raja Gulab Singh, a General in the service of Ranjit Singh, and the individual response for unjustly terrorizing the Kashmiris, collaborated with the British and was given Kashmir as a reward for his assistance.[3] The likes of Gulab would send flour instead of gunpowder to the frontline, misdirect the supply lines, and position Sikh soldiers and artillery where they were not required.

> *"The government of the Sikhs, considered in its theory, may...be termed a theocracy. They obey a temporal chief, it is true; but that chief preserves his power and authority by professing himself the servant of The Khalsa."[4]*

Regrettably, British rule over the Sikh people didn't improve the conditions of the Sikh nation, or Punjab, as the British proliferate. Instead, the Sikh people were pushed backward through time.

Disguised as a beggar, and before the annexation of Punjab, an American named Charles Masson travelled Punjab from 1826 to 1838. He discovered the Sikh Empire as much more prosperous and better administered than British controlled India. Unfortunately, after the British hijacked Punjab, all this changed. For example:

1. There were more literates under Sikh sovereignty than under the British.[5] Under Sikh rule, schools were attached to almost all

Gurudawaras, Hindu Temples, and Mosques (the Sikh Empire was a multi-faith empire). But after annexation, so to dumb the Punjabi, the British actually raided homes and burnt books.[6]

2. Women were encouraged to educate themselves under Sikh sovereignty but the education of women languished under British rule.[7] As observed by the East India Company, the education provided to women by the Sikh Empire was far more advanced than that provided by Europe.

3. Before the British annexed the Sikh Empire, the empire was one of the most educated in the world, as suggested by G.W. Leitner, in his book, *History of Indigenous Education in the Punjab since Annexation and in 1882* (Lahore: Republican Books, 1992). He also emphasizes that the British virtually crippled Punjab's education system.

4. Art, music, and literature were nurtured under Sikh sovereignty[8] but not so much under the Raj.

5. And under the watch of the British, economic policies only increased the hardship and suffering of the people—the financial debts of the poor only grew.[9]

During the reign of the Sikhs, Punjab generated near the same GDP as the entire Mughal Empire, under Emperor Aurangzeb's rule (the richest emperor yet known). At that time, the Mughal Empire covered most of India. But again, after the British took control, Punjab financially suffered. The British stole Punjab's wealth and took it back to England.

In keeping, the British terrorized the people when the people voiced their concerns. For example, in the year 1919, the British purposely murdered and injured thousands of innocent, unarmed, and peaceful civilians.

> *"Jallianwala Bagh. It was here...that one of the most dastardly events of British rule in India took place. On April 13, 1919, Brig.-Gen. Reginald Dyer ordered the brutal massacre...of citizens who had gathered to protest the 'imprisonment without trial' of two of their leaders under the newly passed and unethical Rowlatt Act (similar to the American Patriot Act). Now a leafy garden memorial, the park is surrounded by buildings on all sides, the British officers blocked the only access in and indiscriminately opened fire..."*[10]

Fifty British soldiers, commanded by General Dyer, unloaded 1650 rounds of ammunition into a crowd of 10 000 unarmed Punjabis. The British authorities fully supported the immoral act, and upon arriving back to Britain, General Dyer received a sword inscribed "Saviour of the Punjab".

The 10 000 unarmed were gathered to peacefully protest the Rowlatt Acts (also known as the Black Acts). This British initiative vested the governing body with power to silence the press, detain without trial, and arrest without warrant.

After the savage act, the British also presented Sir Michael O'Dwyer, the Lieutenant Governor of Punjab, and the person who sanctioned Dyer's ungodly actions, with a robe of honour. Sadistically, the British utilized the institution of the Akal Takht (the Sikh Temporal Seat of Authority), through administrators backed by them, to credit O'Dwyer.

The British were able to manipulate a sacred institution as the Akal Takht because the Sikhs were not in control of their institutions. After annexation, the British infiltrated every element of the Sikh culture so to strengthen their power and rule over the Sikh nation. In the process, they readily corrupted Sikh beliefs.

> *"I think it would be politically dangerous to allow the management of the Sikh temples to fall into the hands of a committee emancipated from government control."* —
> Lord Ripon (1881)

Not only did the British manage to violate the temporal philosophy of the Sikhs, they also managed to corrupt their spiritual philosophy.

Under British influence, pictures of Hindu gods were installed in the Gurudawaras and Hindu practices were regularly carried out inside Sikh institutions, practices such as idol worship.[11] In response, the Sikhs organized to retake their sacred places. Under an oath of non-violence, they eventually freed several, but not before the British jailed 30 000 protesters,[12] and not before English officers, police agents, and the corrupt administrators[13] violently attacked those who protested.[14] Nearly 400 were murdered and 2000 injured.[15] They were assaulted as they sat or stood in prayer. Hazara Singh, on January 20th, 1921, in Taran, Taran, was the first victim of the barbaric attack.

Rev. C.F. Andrews witnessed, on one occasion, the brutality and cowardice demonstrated by those attempting to smother the non-violent protests. He writes:

"It was a sight which I never wish to see again, a sight incredible to an Englishman. There were four Akali Sikhs with black turbans facing a band of about a dozen policemen, including two English officers. They had walked slowly upto the line of the police just before I had arrived and they were standing silently in front of them at about a yard's distance. They were perfectly still and did not move further forward. Their hands were placed together in prayer and it was clear that they were praying. Then, without the slightest provocation

on their part, an Englishman lunged forward the head of his 'lathi' which was bound with brass. He lunged it forward in such a way that his fist which held the staff struck the Akali Sikh, who was praying, just at the collar bone with great force. It looked the most cowardly blow as I saw it struck and I had the greatest difficulty in keeping myself under control. But beforehand I had determined that I must, on no account, interfere by word or deed, but simply watch; for the vow which had been taken by the sufferers, must be sacred to me also. Therefore, passive silence on my part was imperative, but it is difficult to describe to those who have not seen the sight with their own eyes how difficult such a passive attitude was. "[16]

"The brutality and inhumanity of the whole scene was indescribably increased by the fact that the men who were hit were praying to God and had already taken a vow that they would remain silent and peaceful in word and deed. The Akali Sikhs who had taken this vow, both at the Golden Temple before starting and also at the shrine of Guru-ka-Bagh were, as I have already stated, largely from the army. They had served in many campaigns in Flanders, in France, in Mesopotamia and in East Africa. Some of them at the risk of their own safety may have saved the lives of Englishmen who had

been wounded. Now they were felled to the ground at the hands of English officials serving in the same Government which they themselves had served. They were obliged to bear the brunt of blows, each one of which was an insult and humiliation, but each blow was turned into a triumph by the spirit with which it was endured.[17]

"What was happening to them was truly, in some dim way, a crucifixion. The Akalis were undergoing their baptism of fire, and they cried to God for help out of the depth of their agony of spirit."[18]

The Sikhs eventually retook some control of their places of worship, but the British did not give the Sikhs complete autonomy—even though the Sikhs believed differently. Before giving what looked like control to the Sikhs, the British persuaded the Sikhs to institute an election system—to determine who should lead the Gurudawaras. The British mixed politics and religion so they might, through the election system, maintain control over the Gurudawaras. This election system still exists, and because of it, the politically savvy are leading the spiritual institutions instead of the spiritually gifted.

But the British's most heinous attack on the Sikh people came in the year 1947. Immediately after World War II, it was clear that British hold over India wouldn't survive the decade. The internal unrest, which was of a peaceful and violent character, would slowly drain their treasury—the British exhausted their finances fighting Hitler. As such, and before they were kicked out, they wisely decided to leave India on their own terms. However, as they were leaving, they partitioned their holdings into two major states, Pakistan and India. In doing so, they divided Punjab into two—one part went to Pakistan and the other to India.

Punjab, for the most part, constituted the Sikh Empire, and after her annexation, believing the empire would be returned to them, the Sikh people were still spread across this territory. The great partition of 1947 left a portion of the Sikh nation in Pakistan and another part in India. As you can imagine, the divide was catastrophic for the Sikh nation.

Firstly, the Sikhs who found themselves on the Pakistan side of the divide were forced by the Muslims to flee to the Indian side. After the divide, factions of the Muslim population declared a holy war (Jihad) against all non-Muslims, which led to the slaughter of hundreds-of-thousands of Sikhs and the injury and displacement of millions.[19]

> *"...militias trawled the countryside for poorly protected villages to raid and raze to the ground, gangs deliberately derailed trains, massacred their passengers one by one or set the carriages ablaze with petrol.*

Women and children were carried away like looted chattels. "[20]

Secondly, the exodus separated the Sikh nation from half their historical and religious heritage, and divided the Sikh holy land into two. Over two hundred sacred pilgrim sites and shrines, most notably, the birthplace of Guru Nanak, were lost to Pakistan.[21]

The British gave important Sikh sites to Pakistan hoping to provoke the Sikhs into fighting with them. As they were leaving, the British were attempting to create conflict within the region. A tactic they employed in almost every nation they were colonizers in.

Thirdly, the Sikhs lost the better developed parts of Punjab to Pakistan. For example, the valuable canal-colony lands were gifted to Pakistan,[22] the most productive and fertile agricultural lands were given to Pakistan,[23] and industrial plants were divorced from the raw materials that sustained them.[24]

Naturally, the economically prosperous Sikhs, who were attached to the territories given to Pakistan,[25] were forced to relinquish their means of generating wealth and influence. The people most able to organize and direct the Sikh nation were crippled.

Fourthly, the divide of 1947 separated the Sikh nation from half her political identity. The Akal Takht, from the time of Guru

Hargobind, and the territory of Lahore, from the time of Ranjit Singh, were the Sikh political capitals,[26] but after the divide, Pakistan took possession of Lahore.

The British, when they annexed Punjab, took the Sikh territory *"as a 'trust' from the last Sikh ruler during his minority."[27]* But staying true to their character, the British broke their word. The promises the British gave were the reasons the Sikhs supported them after annexation. Without Sikh support, thrice, the British would've lost the Jewel of the Empire—during the Mutiny of 1857, WW I, and WW II. Moreover, the Sikhs are considered the Lions of the Great Wars, and it is because of them that Britain survived Hitler. According to Sir Winston Churchill, while speaking to Parliament:

> *"....British people are highly indebted and obliged to Sikhs for a long time, I know that within this century we needed their help twice (referring to the two World Wars) and they did help us very well. As a result of their timely help, we are today able to live with honour, dignity, and independence. In the war, they fought and died for us, wearing the turbans..."*

When it came time to leave India, the British should've returned what they held in trust, but instead, they violated a legal agreement and betrayed the Sikh people. The British didn't even bother to hear the concerns of the Sikhs. The Sikhs were aware of the consequences partition would yield and they aggressively voiced their concerns, but the British ignored them.[28] The British had no intention of leaving the Sikh nation intact[29] and in a state from which it might grow and develop. They even kidnapped the last Maharaja in his infancy and raised him as a European. They raised him on European soil so to remove the head from the body and further alienate the Sikh people from their sense of direction and self-determination. The British were also indoctrinating the child and training him as a British mule, so when the time came for him to govern Punjab, he might be easy to control.

Demonically, even during the massacres of 1947, the British did nothing—*"instead of using...troops to quell the trouble, the British command confined them to barracks and evacuated the men as quickly as they possibly could."*[30] In a letter written to M.A. Jinnah, the Governor of West Punjab (Pakistan), Sir Francis Mudie states, *"I am telling everyone that I don't care how the Sikhs get across the border; the great thing is to get rid of them as soon as possible."*[31]

It isn't that the British weren't aware what partition would do. They fully recognized the radical nature of the Muslims in that area and the neighbouring Islamic regions such as Afghanistan—Afghanies moved into West Punjab and helped cleanse most areas of non-Muslims. The British believed that it would take a miracle for the Sikh nation to survive the partition.[32] But survive the Sikh people did.

The British, during their stay in India and as they were leaving, attempted to destroy the Sikh nation. During their stay, the British tried to destroy the Sikhs so to expand their imperialist ambitions, and because the Sikh culture was an advanced culture. It was important to destroy any advanced cultures the British contacted because, domestically, they pushed the propaganda that they were liberating the people of the world from their inferior cultures. For this type of misinformation to carry weight, the advanced cultures had to be vanished.

If not for British interference, the Sikh nation-state would have advanced as the Europeans and grown powerful enough to conquer her neighbours. It should not be missed that the Sikh Empire believed strongly in art, music, literature, science, mathematics, logic, engineering, architecture, spirituality, morality, ethics, European technology, European knowledge, European innovation, European administration, and European management. Europeans were readily employed by the Sikh nation-state.[33] For this reason, the Khalsa was the most formidable fighting force on the continent. They wisely combined European knowledge with the philosophy of a Saint-Soldier.

With this in mind, as the British were leaving, in collaboration with the Hindu elite, the Brits created circumstances to cripple the Sikh nation. Now, why would they do something like this? Well, I believe they did it for four principle reasons.

1) They wish to one day reclaim their status as an empire and it's easier to eliminate a potential rival before that potential comes to light.

2) Sikhie presents a direct challenge to Christianity and Sikhie has the potential to reduce the Christian count—reducing the influence of those who use the Christian institutions to motivate and mobilize the people. The British relied heavily on the Christian religion to motivate their people to occupy others and further their imperialistic ambitions.

3) If the Sikh nation regained her sovereignty and rebuilt her advanced culture, the British people might realize that they were lied to and British colonial motivations were not as benevolent.

4) And the Second World War significantly reduced the British Armed Forces. The British were in need of soldiers. With the destruction of the Sikh Empire, the British were able to retain the Sikh soldiers already members of their military. The Sikhs were their greatest military asset. *"They were recognised by the British as some of the best fighting men in the country."*[34] An English observer once wrote, *"As for the bravery and warlike spirit of the Sikhs, no Cossack, no Turk, no Russian, can measure swords with*

them."[35] For example, at the Battle of Saragarhi, Sept. 12th, 1897, 21 Sikh soldiers, to the last man, battled 10 000 Afghans.

The British admired the zeal of the Khalsa so much that some of their officials argued for the Christian Church to be just as passionate and faithful, and for the British to incorporate the Khalsa into the Christian fold.[36] So long as the Singhs could be ruled over.

After annexation, the Sikhs initially supported the British because the Sikhs were fooled into thinking they were equal to the British and free. Not only this, the British promised to return the Sikh Empire. The first generation or two of Sikhs fell victim to the propaganda and assisted the Crown. But by the turn of the century, some Sikhs realized the truth behind British rule. For example, in the year 1909, former British-Sikh soldiers living in Vancouver, Canada, protested against British discrimination by torching their military uniforms and the medals they received as British soldiers. For which Bhai Bhag Singh, the person who inspired the protest, was shot by a British agent.[37]

You might be wondering why the Hindu elite collaborated. Well, the Hindu ruling class worked hand-in-hand with the British. More importantly, the British permitted the elite to be elite. If the Hindu ruling class didn't do what the British dictated, the British would remove them and create a new ruling class. For this reason, the

British were able to maintain control over such a large population by means of a few—relatively speaking.

The Hindu elite also collaborated so to prevent the Sikh philosophy from dominating India and erasing the caste system—a system that empowers and enriches the Hindu elite. The Sikh philosophy teaches of equality and a higher standard of living for all—regardless of a person's place in the Hindu caste system. If such a thing as the caste system fell, as would the people who benefit from the divisions. Think about it, some of the richest people in the world are from India. Why is this? It's because they exploit the poor people. A worker makes pocket change while their masters make millions a day.

Even still, the Hindu dominated Indian Government attacks the Sikh people. For example, from the year 1984 to 1992, the Indian military murdered over 250 000 Sikhs.

After much hardship and countless battles, the Sikh people defeated the Mughal Empire, and then the Afghan invaders, to create their own kingdom. Unfortunately, the British imperial agenda could not permit a noble and advanced nation to exist, the British could not help but eye the Sikh Empire's resources, and the British agenda beckoned to control as much of the earth as possible—regardless of who stood in the way. As such, they destroyed the empire of the

Saint-Soldier in their ungodly attempts to fulfill their ungodly ambitions.

....

In 1984, the British Government, under Prime Minister Margaret Thatcher, again attacked the Sikh culture. They assisted the Indian Government in their assault on the Sikh people by providing the Indian military with equipment, logistics, manpower, consultation, and training.

The Brutish British: Endnotes

1) Pritam Singh, Federalism, Nationalism and Development: India and the Punjab Economy (Routledge: New York, NY, 2008), p. 30.

2) William Wilson Hunter, The Indian Empire: its people, history and products, 2nd edition (Trübner , 1886), p. 411. [http://www.google.com/books?id=P3cIAAAAQAAJ&dq=A+Brief +history+of+the+Indian+People]

3) Vivek Chadha, Low Intensity Conflict in India (Sage Publications: New Delhi: India, 2005), p. 172.

4) John Malcolm, Sketch of the Sikhs (J. Murray, 1812), p.114. [http://www.google.com/books?id=GMUKAAAAYAAJ&dq=Sketc h+of+the+Sikhs]

5) G.S. Chabra, Advanced Study in the History of Modern India (Lotus Press: New Delhi, 2005), p. 137.

6) Ibid., p. 138.

7) J.S. Grewal, The Sikhs of the Punjab (Cambridge University Press: Cambridge, UK, 1998), p. 111.

8) Martin E. Marty and R.Scott Appleby, Fundamentalisms Observed (University of Chicago Press: United States, 1994), p. 1.

9) Pritam Singh, Federalism, Nationalism and Development: India and the Punjab Economy (Routledge: New York, NY, 2008), p. 29.

10) Keith Bain, Niloufer Venkatraman and Pippa de Bruyn, Frommer's India 2nd edition (Wiley Publishing: Hoboken, New Jersey, 2006), p. 465.

11) Pritam Singh, Federalism, Nationalism and Development: India and the Punjab Economy (Routledge: New York, NY, 2008), p. 30.

12) Cynthia Keppley Mahmood, Fighting for Faith and Nation: dialogues with Sikh militants (University of Pennsylvania Press: Philadelphia, 1997), p. 112.

13) Pritam Singh, Federalism, Nationalism and Development: India and the Punjab Economy (Routledge: New York, NY, 2008), p. 30.

14) Martin E. Marty and R.Scott Appleby, Fundamentalisms Observed (University of Chicago Press: United States, 1994), p. 608.

15) Cynthia Keppley Mahmood, Fighting for Faith and Nation: dialogues with Sikh militants (University of Pennsylvania Press: Philadelphia, 1997), p. 112.

16) Bakhshish Singh Nijjar, History of the United Panjab, Volume 1 (Atlantic Publishers and Distributors: New Delhi, 1996), p. 99-100.

17) Ibid., p. 101.

18) Ibid., p. 99.

19) Thomas R. Metcalf, <u>A Concise History of Modern India</u> (Cambridge University Press: United States, 2001), p. 88.

20) Yasmin Khan, <u>The Great Partition: the making of India and Pakistan</u> (Yale University Press: United States, 2007), p. 128.

21) Cynthia Keppley Mahmood, <u>Fighting for Faith and Nation: dialogues with Sikh militants</u> (University of Pennsylvania Press: Philadelphia, 1996), p. 114.

22) Gyanesh Kudaisya and Tai Yong Tan, <u>The Aftermath of Partition in South Asia: volume 3 of Routledge studies in the modern history of Asia</u> (Routledge: London; New York, 2000), p. 101.

23) Vivek Chadha, <u>Low Intensity Conflicts In India: an analysis</u> (Sage Publications of India: New Delhi, India, 2005), p. 186.

24) Yasmin Khan, <u>The Great Partition: the making of India and Pakistan</u> (Yale University Press: United States, 2007), p. 126.

25) Vivek Chadha, <u>Low Intensity Conflicts In India: an analysis</u> (Sage Publications of India: New Delhi, India, 2005), p. 186.

26) Ibid.

27) Cynthia Keppley Mahmood, <u>Fighting for Faith and Nation: dialogues with Sikh militants</u> (University of Pennsylvania Press: Philadelphia, 1996), p. 113.

28) Ibid.

29) Gyanesh Kudaisya and Tai Yong Tan, The Aftermath of Partition in South Asia: volume 3 of Routledge studies in the modern history of Asia (Routledge: London; New York, 2000), p. 101 -124.

30) Yasmin Khan, The Great Partition: the making of India and Pakistan (Yale University Press: United States, 2007), p. 128.

31) Raj Pal Singh, The Sikhs: their journey of five hundred years (Bhavana Books and Prints: New Delhi, 2003), p. 274.

32) Gyanesh Kudaisya and Tai Yong Tan, The Aftermath of Partition in South Asia: volume 3 of Routledge studies in the modern history of Asia (Routledge: London; New York, 2000), p. 117.

33) Khushwant Singh, Ranjit Singh: Maharaja of the Punjab (Penguin Books: India, 2001) p. 139-148.

34) Vivek Chadha, Low Intensity Conflicts In India: an analysis (Sage Publications of India: New Delhi, India, 2005), p. 169.

35) Max Arthur McAuliffe, The Sikh Religion, Volume 1 (Forgotten Books, 2008), p. 11.
[http://www.google.com/books?id=E0UwOOjrjGAC&dq=The+Sikh+Religion]

36) John Malcolm Ludlow, <u>British India, Its Race and Its History Considered with Reference to the Mutinies of 1857: a series of lectures addressed to the students of the working men's college</u> (Cambridge: Macmillan and Co, 1858), p. 307.
[http://www.google.com/books?id=bGQOAAAAQAAJ&dq=The+History+of+the+Sikhs:+together+with+a+concise+account+of+the+Punjab+and+Cashmere]

37) Gurpreet Singh, "Forgotten event that changed the course of history." <u>Apna Roots</u>, October 9th, 2009.

CHAPTER 2
PEACEKEEPERS?

Blood Rain

War is a pricey business. The cost to train a killer and to purchase military technology has driven nations into extreme debt, and the debt can double when the cost to rebuild the devastated country is attached.

A war indebts a nation, and after all the bloodshed paints the soil red and evaporates, the only that seem to profit are the bankers and the banks.

War is a benefit to the bankers and the banks. Regardless of the outcome, they profit from the money lent. And the bigger and the longer the war, the more money is advanced. More importantly for them, a higher loan translates into higher interest payments. If a nation borrows more than they annually take in, eventually, the nation will reach a financial crisis. In which a nation is unable to make payments toward the principle and only able to pay the annual interest. When this is a reality, a nation is at the mercy of the banks and the bankers and their ideological direction—no matter if it's immoral, unethical, or selfish.

Banks and bankers profit when nations war and they care little for who emerges the victor. Typically, banks and bankers finance all sides, even those who make the weapons, and losing is rarely the outcome for them. They are the true masters of the chessboard— amid kings, presidents, and prime ministers, they are emperors.

God Bless the Dead

> *Let's not fool ourselves, the liberty G.W Bush propagated is nowhere to be found and yesterday's civilian is tomorrow's freedom-fighter.*

Every day, more and more innocent people in Afghanistan, and by extension, the Muslim world, are starting to harbour a dislike for the West. But in the West, the story isn't told as such.

The narrative is occasionally fraudulent, as such, the Westerner doesn't read, hear, or see the plight of the innocent Afghan (in no way do I refer to Al Qaeda, the Taliban, ISIL, or any other terrorist organization). In the West, the people have no idea that more and more people are turning against them.

Now, don't get me wrong, the Afghans desire freedom as much as we would if we suffered at the hands of the Taliban, but freedom isn't what the Allies are giving. If freedom is and was given, then more than half the Afghans wouldn't want the Allies disappeared.[1]

The anti-West sentiment is growing because the allied forces do not take the time and the care to distinguish who's who. If they did, they wouldn't randomly invade homes hoping to find a terrorist.[2] If they did, they wouldn't bomb entire districts within villages because they thought a terrorist was somewhere there hiding. If they did, they wouldn't have "accidentally" bombed a wedding procession.[3] If they did, they wouldn't have tortured and murdered 3000 POWs.[4]

And if they did, the civilian death toll wouldn't be as high as it is—thousands upon thousands of innocent civilians have perished.[5]

The Allies are reckless, as if the invasion was a video game and "the reset button" was an option, but the people in the West aren't privy to this perspective. In the West, the story is illustrated to depict the nation of Afghanistan as home to more terrorists than civilians. But the fact of the matter is, before the invasion of Afghanistan, the terrorists were a small percentage of the population, and of them, many were not Afghan. The people in the West don't seem to comprehend this, and blame I do those who cater the information a person uses to formulate their opinion.

It's more than evident that the Alliance needs a change in attitude, as John Hancock did in the movie starring Will Smith. The liberation of Afghanistan from the Taliban was a good idea but the collateral damage is counterproductive and godless.

Thousands of innocent civilians were murdered including the elderly, women, and children.[6] What this means is thousands of hearts were broken, thousands of tears were kept in, thousands of fists were held back, and thousands of new enemies were made. It should come as no surprise to hear that those who once had no quarrel with the Alliance are now turning against them.[7] In their minds, the distinction between the Alliance and the Taliban is slowly disappearing. And can we really blame them? Are they not responding as any people would? Wouldn't we do the same if a foreign power came into our country and started murdering the innocent? I think even the pacifists would desire revenge, and I guarantee our blood would boil as theirs if one of our family members was unjustly slain. I think we too would change our occupation from a civilian to a freedom-fighter. But the story isn't depicted accurately. As such, the audience is unaware of the innocent Afghan's plight, and the developed nations—through their military—murder and breed hate for their respective nations.

Hypothetically speaking, if one of the many Afghans, who lost a family member to the bullet of a Western soldier, manages to retaliate by bombing a major Western city, what will happen then? Will the ideas of right and wrong further distort as they did in America after 9/11? Instead of recognizing the root of the problem, the audience might adopt the mentality of an innocent victim and harbour a want for revenge, just as the Americans did. A phenomenon I call the twin-tower effect. If this ever happens, the cycle of hate will begin its second rotation, and generations from now, each side will view the other as the evil and each side will work to satisfy the want for revenge. The root, generations from now, will have burrowed too deep for mere human hands to unearth.

The cycle of hate is potentially seeded but the story isn't told as such, and the Westerner doesn't read, hear, or see the plight of the innocent Afghan.

Mike Bhangu

God Bless the Dead: Endnotes

1. Robert Greenwald, Director, *Rethink Afghanistan*, 2009.

2. Ibid.

3. "Troops in Contact: Airstrikes and Civilian Deaths in Afghanistan." September 8, 2008. Human Rights Watch. [http://www.hrw.org/en/reports/2008/09/08/troops-contact-0], accessed January, 2009.

4. Jamie Doran, Director, *Afghan Massacre: Convoy of Death*, 2002.

5. "Civilian causalities of war in Afghanistan (2001 - Present)." Wikipedia. [http://en.wikipedia.org/wiki/Civilian_casualties_of_the_War_in_Af ghanistan_(2001%E2%80%93present)], accessed January, 2009.

6. "Afghanistan Conflict Monitor." Human Security Report Project. [http://www.afghanconflictmonitor.org/civilian_casualties/index.htm l], accessed January, 2009. / "Afghan Archives: Civilian Casualties." War Report. [http://www.comw.org/warreport/afghanarchiveciv.html], accessed January, 2009.

7. "Troops in Contact: Airstrikes and Civilian Deaths in Afghanistan." September 8, 2008. Human Rights Watch. [http://www.hrw.org/en/reports/2008/09/08/troops-contact-0], accessed January, 2009.

How to Lose an Empire

Honour is as honour does... regardless if the war-makers know or not.

During the colonial age, much darkness was released, and the light of the planet was transformed into a flicker from a flame.

The dark reality unleashed by the colonial demons still ripples and there are lessons to be learned here. First and foremost, darkness can never defeat light and an empire built by the shadows of the devil is an empire destined to fall. Proven this history has and even the colonialists could not defy this Universal axiom.

Empires begin their decline soon after they adopt an oppressive attitude towards the people they occupy. You see, most people are hesitant to act violent and most people would rather spend their time with their family and friends eating, laughing, and playing. Most people will endure the occupier for as long as they can but every person has a breaking point. Take peace, freedom, and happiness from the people and they will fight.

Eventually, people will act violent so to secure some sort of peace, freedom, and happiness, no matter how the violence is depicted within the home-nation of the occupier, and regardless if the media attached the word "irrational" or "senseless" to their behaviour.

The term "irrational" or "senseless" doesn't change the facts, and sometimes, it's better to discard the prescribed vision and squint to see the truth.

Honour is as honour does... regardless if the war-makers know or not. So, if wishing to maintain and expand an empire, behave as Jesus. If acting as an evil archetype, watch an empire explode into pieces.

I Stand on Guard for Thee

This is a letter I wrote many years ago. It's addressed to the Canadian Prime Minister responsible for sanctioning an offensive Canadian military presence in a country not Canada.

God bless the Canadian soldiers who died in Afghanistan. I write with no intent to disrespect them and I write to ask my government why they sent them. Why are we participating in the occupation of another people and their nation? Why are we participating in the torture of the Afghan and the murder of the innocent? Mr. Chicken-Hawk, I thought we were better than such ugly and ungodly motions. Mr. Chicken-Hawk, I thought we were Canadian.

Mr. Chicken-Hawk, I heard your political spin and it sounded akin to what G.W. Bush said on CNN before you were elected. Let me guess, you thought you could fool us Canadians just as he did the Americans. Well, Mr. Chicken-Hawk, understand this, war is not a part of a Canadian's nature and nothing you can say will make it.

Mr. Chicken-Hawk, war isn't a part of a Canadian's nature and proven this Canadians have, but the positive associations Canadians worked so hard to make are under attack because of your behaviour on the international scene. I'm a proud Canadian but I wonder how proud the world will be of me after we mutate into a warring nation? I wonder if they'll mistake me for an American? Mr. Chicken-Hawk, do you know what it is to be a Canadian? Last time I checked, war wasn't one of our characteristics.

Mr. Chicken-Hawk, do you understand Canadian characteristics, can you comprehend how the world operates behind a veil of a realist, or can I call you a cardboard box politician?

Let me ask Mr. Chicken-Hawk—Have you spoken to a people who were occupied by the British and the other colonialists? Colonial actions are despised with a passion and half the world remembers them as thieves, murderers, and extortionists. Mr. Chicken-Hawk, did you not learn from past mistakes?

Please, let me in on your vision. I ask—Is it the same one I have for my nation? I see a people who build an example and emancipate the many races. I see a people who build a home respectful of the many faiths and faces. I see a people who show the world how to peacefully live. Mr. Chicken-Hawk, do you see through the same prescription glasses?

....
World renowned peace-keepers no more?

BBP acknowledges the support of the Canada Council for the Arts, which last year invested $153 million to bring the arts to Canadians throughout the country.

Nous remercions le Conseil des arts du Canada de son soutien. L'an dernier, le Conseil a investi 153 millions de dollars pour mettre de l'art dans la vie des Canadiennes et des Canadiens de tout le pays.

Made in the USA
Middletown, DE
11 December 2019